GAGE'S FIRST D████████

WRITTEN BY:

DR. JOSH FARR

ILLUSTRATED BY:

OUMAYMA MHIRI

DEDICATION:

This book is dedicated to my Pap Farr and Dad, the men who blessed me with their time by sharing their love of the great outdoors and especially hunting.

Gage was excited to go hunting for the first time. Ever since he could remember, it had been a family tradition that his Dad and Grandpa would go out whitetail hunting after Thanksgiving.

They told him that they would take him out when he turned 8. Gage loved hearing about all of their adventures, but most of all, he loved practicing shooting with his Grandpa and taking long walks in the woods.

No one knew how much shooting practice mattered more than Gage did as they walked through the woods on this cold opening day of deer season in late November.

Gage felt so prepared with his rifle slung over his shoulder just in case an animal came out unexpectedly from behind some trees or bushes.

Gage, Dad, and Grandpa got to their hunting spot just as daylight began. It was located on the edge of a field and near the woods. "This is a great place where we have been seeing deer each day," said Grandpa.

This hunting spot was a few trees that had fallen over, and Dad and Grandpa put out chairs behind it. It seemed perfect because it could hide everyone from the deer while still allowing all to see the whole field and all the woods' edge.

It wasn't long before they heard
rustling around them - a deer!
Gage was so excited and nervous that
he quickly pulled up his rifle at the deer.
Gage took aim at it and shot - but missed!
The deer ran away.

It all happened so quickly that Dad and Grandpa didn't get time to shoot at the deer.
They wanted to see Gage get his first shot. Gage was upset, but his Grandpa told him, "Everyone misses; that it is a part of hunting and it happens to the best of us."

Gage was anxious to see more deer, but they did not see more deer for quite some time. After having lunch, they decided to try a new spot.

It wasn't long after lunch.
"I can't believe it!" Gage exclaimed.
"We've been out here for hours and not
seen any more deer! I'm so mad."

Gage's Grandpa sighed, patting him on the back. "It happens to everyone. You'll get the hang of this, just give it some time. That is why they call this sport hunting, and not shooting, Gage."

"But I don't want to wait," Gage said grumpily. He was feeling quite defeated at this point, and he really wanted something good to happen before they went home.

Every year Gage heard about all of the fun hunting stories between Dad and Grandpa. Each year they would come home with deer, and it would provide many good snacks throughout the year.

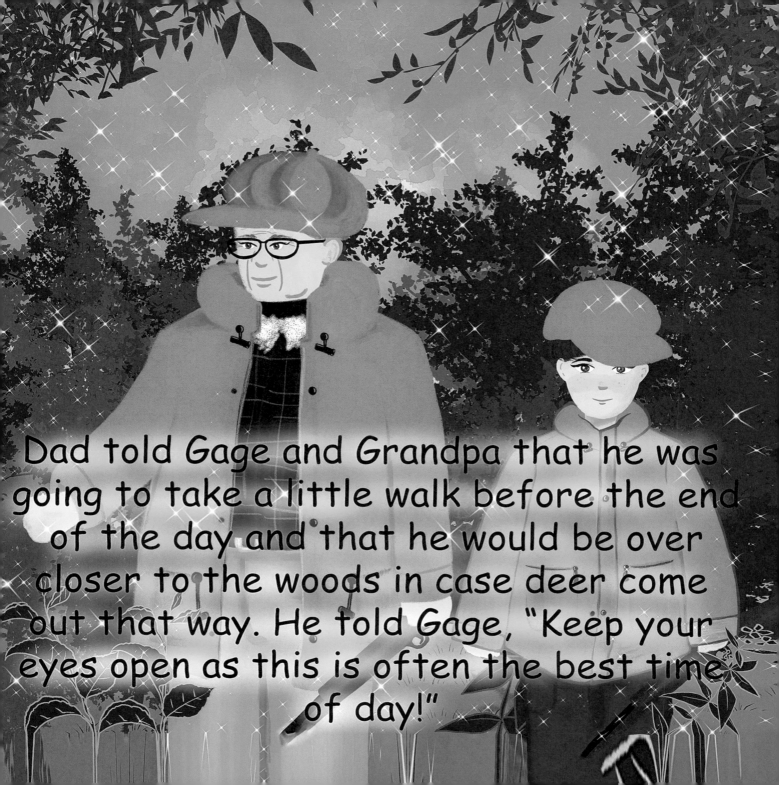

Dad told Gage and Grandpa that he was going to take a little walk before the end of the day and that he would be over closer to the woods in case deer come out that way. He told Gage, "Keep your eyes open as this is often the best time of day!"

The sun had begun its descent in the sky- no doubt signaling that their hunting expedition would soon be over for another day. Suddenly there was rustling from behind them! Heart racing with excitement and adrenaline, Gage was anxious about what it could be. There were only a few minutes left of hunting time, and could it be that this would be an unlucky day for them?

Suddenly, behind the brush, a whitetail deer walked out in front of them. Grandpa told Gage to take his time and to move his gun up into position.

Gage waited for the deer to slowly put its head down to eat and waited for the deer to turn completely towards them. Gage then pulled the trigger!

Bam!! The gun went off, and the deer disappeared from where it was standing. Gage thought for sure he missed another deer and quickly become sad that all of his hard work into practice shooting and trying to shoot a deer wasn't paying off. Grandpa told Gage, "Wait a minute and then we will go up and check where you shot."

Gage's dad began walking over to Gage and Grandpa, from where he was seated. He quickly yelled, "Gage, you got it!!"

Grandpa and Gage couldn't see the deer, but they ran up to where Dad was standing. Sure enough, the deer lie there. Gage was so happy!!!

Grandpa and Dad both gave Gage a high five and congratulated him on his first deer!
Grandpa said to Gage, "This certainly will be a memory that you will never forget."

As the years passed and hunting season come around each year, Gage remembered his first deer. To this day, he hunts and enjoys the outdoors with new friends and family and continues to make new memories that will last a lifetime.

to be continued...

Made in the USA
Columbia, SC
09 November 2023

25547554R00024